GLOWSTICK

Jade M. Wong

Dear Melody,

Thank you for coming ✷

Don't forget to shine ♥

GLOWSTICK

Cover Art & Layout: Fabha Sulthana

ISBN: 978-1-7373164-0-4

Introduction

I have loved words since I could speak and read, or maybe even before then. Maybe I was born filled with words I could not yet understand but knew they would be important someday. When my childhood faded away, words became my escape from the struggle of living, my lantern warding off unwanted shadows, and my curious contemplation that maybe I wasn't alone.

What if there were others living in limbo? What if there were others who understood being strong didn't mean we were invincible, but rather, it meant we felt our pain and chose to concentrate on the beauty within? And what if someone was out there with a hole inside their chest they didn't know how to fill, their only solution to lie in the dark and wait for the emptiness to end, as I still do from time to time?

What if I could help?

To you reading this—I don't know if these words will do for you what so many words have done for me. I do know depression is misunderstood as a looming cloud of eternal sadness when in reality, there are rays of light that pierce through the cloud, providing little moments of peace. That's the cruelness of depression. You can get a reprieve from the rain only to drown in the storm. Still, I'm hoping you'll join me on this raft made of letters and ink.

To you reading this—please know words have taken me out of the shadows and into the light, even if that light flickers from time to time. So, I pass these words on to you, in hopes you will pass them on to someone who may find them helpful. Together, maybe we can be each other's glowstick in the dark.

With Love,
Jade

The Beginnings of a Story

Brimming with ideas,
But the page was blank.
Words floated to the surface,
Then once more they sank.

A twitch of the pen,
A spark in the mind,
And the words flew free
Leaving doubt behind.

Once an empty page,
Now painted with glory,
And brimming with
The beginnings of a story.

This Is My Story

This is a story of how I lived.
My memories with those closest to me
A story apiece and through them relived
All the days we were so carefree,

The days when a scraped knee
Or a heart broken by a boy
Swayed my world
Between anguish and joy,

I always thought I had more time
I didn't plan it and I don't know why
One day I left my body behind
This is a story of how I died.

Bleed

Writing is like sex—it's messy, it's fun, we put words down on paper in any which way that turns us on and intrigues us.

Bringing the story to life is like giving birth—it's tough, it's excruciating, we willingly endure the pain and realization that our long nights and early mornings will never be the same.

To give birth to the story, we bleed. We cut ourselves wide open because our blood pumping through our veins is how we know we're alive and pumping blood through the veins of our words is how they come to life.

Right now, I can't stop the bleeding.

A Beautiful Cage

It was a beautiful cage that glittered and shone.
Embellished with diamonds, a spectacle to own,
It was adorned in carvings woven in thread
Of emerald and ruby in the richest red.

Inside the cage was a padded mattress
As soft as a cloud, fit for a goddess,
And on the mattress, there sat a creature—
A creature who yearned to see and discover

A view of the world from a tall mountain peak,
Or a peek at the ocean deep with mystique,
A view of adventure, of horizons stretched far,
A view of anything beyond the diamond bars.

Almost Lovers

Her feet dangled over the side of the bridge,
tapping the sturdy bricks to a tune only she heard.
An intricate braid hung down her back, strands of
black interwoven with lilac. She wore a lavender
dress with lacy hems that flowed to her knees and
accentuated the color in her hair. She was a violet
vision, and I couldn't look away.

All at once, I saw our future bloom in my mind.
Her giggling over Saturday morning pancakes as I
dab maple syrup on her nose. Love notes tucked
inside her lunch to surprise her during work.
Maybe she was a beloved teacher or perhaps a
professional artist who kept her personal life quiet.

I decided to introduce myself right before I
watched her stand and step off the bridge,
breaking the surface of the water, purple colliding
with blue.

It was her serene face framed by lilac bangs that
would appear in my dreams for years after. If I had
decided to introduce myself a second earlier,
could I have saved my almost lover?

For Them

This poem

Is for the child
Sprinting through the crimson streets
Tripping over the last breaths
Of his father—

For the mother
Protecting her babies' ears
From the piercing shrieks that echo
Long after the ashes settle—

For the thousands of eyes
That look to the sky
Through acid and smoke
And never look back down.

Bubble

I was born without wings,
　　　　I was not meant to fly.
　　　　A small little thing,
　　　　Not meant for the sky.

I was born in a bubble,
　　　　And kept out of trouble.
　　　　I was taught to smile,
　　　　Like an obedient child.

I saw them with their wings,
　　　　Red and gold jeweled things.
　　　　I watched them as they passed.
　　　　Like dazzling colored glass.

I watched them all soar,
　　　　And dip with the breeze,
　　　　I watched them all fly,
　　　　Wherever they pleased.

And all this time,
　　　　I watched them shine,
　　　　For I was a small little thing
　　　　With no wings of mine.

I Dream of Wings

I envision my wings in my mind's eye. When I fall asleep, they stretch and unfurl magnificently at my side. In my dreams, I leap from glittering skyscrapers and let the wind carry me high above the lights. I glide in and out of shadows, savoring the coolness of the night.

It's always just a dream.

I wonder—if I woke up one day and sprouted wings, would everyone stare at me? Would they whisper in awe or back away in fear? Would they *tsk* and tell me to get my head out of the clouds? Or would they not notice at all because if I sprouted wings, then I would have already flown away.

The Me She Never Had

I see her lying on the bed,
Groaning, stumbling, words unsaid.
First to stir and last to sleep,
I see the tears her body weeps.

She does it all with an aching heart,
Oh, how words have torn us apart.
Yet always, always, I hear her voice,
Strained but sharp among the noise.

I see her eyes huddled and sad,
Longing for the me she never had.
I hear the sighs as she trudges on,
Pieces of our hearts, torn and gone.

Sunsets

Red and gold, orange and rose, I see the world in sunsets. In the bareness of the day, in its bright unyielding gaze, I squirm and look away. Some days, I am more defiant, and I stare at the light with a challenge in my eyes. I always lose.

They say, with every sunset there is a sunrise that follows, that every night ushers in a new dawn. They also say the sun, though a magnificent star, will eventually die. So, won't there be one sunset with no sunrise?

Red and gold, orange and rose, cerulean blue and dark indigo, I see the world in sunsets.

Ashes

I wandered in the darkness, fingers outstretched, hoping to feel you there. Like a little girl afraid of the dark, I reached out for the safety of your hand, but all I touched was dust.

If I were truly honest with myself, then I would confess that I knew you would never be the one to lead me out of the dark. For so long, I tried desperately to disperse the doubts, to scatter them as I would scatter ashes into the wind. The wind, however, tends to blow back to you, what you threw into it.

This morning, the wind caressed my face. It was cold, chilly, and full of ashes, but it whispered to me what I always knew. I always knew the way out.

Gone

Past the sound of falling water,
Hidden behind the dark curtain of my hair,
I cried.
I spoke to you in quiet sobs,
Hoping you'll pause where you are,
Look up and wonder inside—

When was the last time I heard her laugh?
Has it really been so long?
Should I hug her a little tighter tonight?
Because tomorrow she might be gone.

Attention

"Did she talk to you?"
"Did she say something to you?"
They shook their heads blankly.
"Why not?"
"Why didn't she say anything?"
They asked each other softly.

The truth was she was scared
To speak out about her demons,
Scared they would not understand,
Or say she sought attention.

And maybe that wasn't good enough
Of a reason to stay silent,
Maybe she couldn't bring herself
To burden those she loved,
And maybe, to her chaotic mind,
There was bravery in staying quiet.

Irresistible

He was irresistible to me
Because he tasted of freedom and I
Was a dove with broken wings.

Follow Your Heart

Do what makes you happy. Stay true to yourself.

How does she follow her heart when her heart is turning in circles? How does she stay true to herself when they all tell her she's wrong?

When they're all sleeping soundly, they don't know that a young woman is on the other side of the door, muffling the sounds of her tears. She lies awake, hands over her mouth as she sobs into her pillow. She forces herself to stop the tears, but seconds later they fall again.

There is so much regret in her heart and every day, she locks yet another regret away. She didn't mean to say those words. She didn't mean to be so different. She's not the person they think she is. She doesn't know how to be what they want.

She no longer knows who she is and maybe that is why she cries.

Are You Listening?

Can you hear me?
All the words I cannot speak
Behind a strained smile sewed on
Like a porcelain doll.

Can you hear me?
The muffled sobs in a corner
Because my tears would only
Burn them like acid rain.

Can you hear me?
Screaming until I shatter
Into pieces of broken glass
Streaked with blood and no reflection.

Can you hear me?
Pleading for your help
To ease the burden of a little girl
To ease her silent pain.

Freedom

That girl walks free, but there's a sadness in her eyes. It's a sadness that lingers in every part of her body. It's a sadness beyond tears or pain. It's a sadness that comes from emptiness.

The sadness crawls down her spine, paralyzing, debilitating. It settles in her shoulder blades, hunched over until exhausted, she can't look up. It runs free in her mind, shattering the chains she desperately throws at it.

That girl walks free, but sadness shackles her inside.

A Wish Fulfilled

Once upon a time, there lived a girl whose only wish was to see the world.

She dreamed of grand castles crumbling past their time, of wandering their hallways and discovering their secrets. She dreamed of diving in deep blue waters, of swimming with the dolphins as they followed the coral to the other side of the ocean. She dreamed of hiking mountains, higher and higher until she could poke her head through the clouds.

That girl dreamed so earnestly that, one night, her dreams tapped on her bedroom window and invited her to join them.

"Come with us!" they exclaimed. *"All you have to do is hold on to us and jump. Don't worry, you'll land among the stars."*

That girl stretched out her hand and let her dreams carry her away.

Some say she is still dreaming, never looking back since she left that night. Others say she came back once to say a proper goodbye to her parents and her brother and her cousins and her friends. They say when she returned, there were so many people to greet her, so many people who wanted to wish her well, it was like the whole world showed up.

Chains

He wanted a girl with pearls,
    But all I had were chains.
He wanted to feel the sun,
    But all I felt was pain.

He left to find a girl who was happy,
    And I am alone again.

Sea of Sad Songs

Stranded
With no land in sight,
Perhaps it's better to sink.

Straining
To hear past the noise
Of every thought I think.

Once
You were my life raft,
My reason to be strong.

Now
I wonder how long it'll take
To drown in this sea of sad songs.

Swords

Day in, day out, their painful words stab and draw blood from every angle. You try to bottle up all their words, but they settle on your lungs like bricks, solid and heavy. You stumble from dizziness as their words clog your arteries, stopping blood and oxygen from reaching your brain.

You fall…

Lying on the ground, blood dripping, gasping for air, the last thing you see is the crowd of people looming over you, their words glinting like blood-tipped swords.

Blame

You watched our colors fade to gray.
You didn't understand why I walked away.
You thought me heartless as I turned my back,
As the blood seeped through the cracks.

You grabbed my arm, livid, and said,
It was my fault our love was now dead.
I jerked out of your grasp and said,
"Will you take the blame for all the times I bled?"

Dangerous

I don't know when I decided
To burn instead of shine,
To be a typhoon instead of a wave.

Maybe I decided
When you broke this heart of mine,
And buried the pieces in a grave.

His fellow officers bustled around the room, but it was quiet to him, as if the walls themselves held their breaths and watched him with invisible eyes.

His own hazel eyes scanned the home. The black leather couch looked comfortable, the colorful pillows adding a whimsical touch. A basket of fruit filled with bright red apples sat atop the dining table. Keys laid on the spindly table by the front door, attached to a miniature stuffed panda bear keychain.

After several steps into the apartment, he noticed the first sign. On the dining table, initially obscured by the fruit basket, was a half-filled mug of ginger tea. The second sign was on the floor outside the kitchen. Fluffy slippers pointed towards a bedroom, as if someone took them off midway and simply kept walking.

Hand on the bedroom doorknob, he knocked out of courtesy and habit. Then, remembering why he was here, he slowly pushed the door open.

She lay in her bed, still in her pajamas, eyes closed and hands folded on her chest. She looked so serene. For a moment, he hoped she was only sleeping but her face, once vibrant with rosy cheeks, was now pale like an angel drained of color. Under her palms, she held a piece of paper to her body.

They told him, *"the first one is always the worst, but eventually you learn to manage your emotions."*

He never learned to manage. He never learned to forget a face, a name, or a life. He always expected to find the city frozen at moments like these because surely, the world would have realized someone important was gone, someone we should have done a better job protecting. He never understood how people could forget so easily.

Someone handed him a piece of paper and he forced his eyes to focus.

Date of birth…

She was only twenty-five years old.

Reunion

I close my eyes
That are finally dry
And tilt my face to the sky.

I feel the wind
I can finally smile
Knowing one day you and I

Will meet again
The wind will blow
My ashes to where you lie.

I spread my arms
The wind begins
I am ready to fly.

It

It haunts me every day,
It haunts me every night,
When my eyes are wide open,
It blocks out all the light.

It whispers in my ear,
It whispers in my head,
When my memory starts to fade,
It makes sure I never forget.

I can feel it in my bones,
I can feel it in my soul,
With every passing second,
I can feel it take its toll.

Today it is merciless,
But I don't know its name.
The only thing I know is
That all days feel the same.

In My Head

Just choose to be happy. It's all in your head.

They called her weak for succumbing to her mind, they said she didn't try hard enough. They claimed it was fake, she didn't want to change, and she was making it all up. When she slept all day and missed all her meals, they said she was lazy and unmotivated.

"If she wanted to eat, she would," they said. *"This is a life she's created."*

But for all the criticism they spewed her way, they never looked inside her. If they did, they would have noticed a brain unlike most others. She had a brain that was darker than others, it didn't light up like it was supposed to. A brain that never stopped clawing at her, that trapped her in a fortress she could not break through.

Yes, this darkness was in her head and it was real to the end.

Chase of Fear

The thunder wails in unleashed anguish.
    The wind howls in a duet.
    The heavens cry teardrops of sorrow,
    As I run, panting and wet.

A creeping fear that clings to my soul,
    My heart pounds like a deafening drum.
    In the darkest of nights, you chase me.
    In the hours of midnight, I run.

The feel of wet grass on my cheek,
    Tears of dread, of final defeat,
    I shut my eyes, I will not confront
    A demon that doesn't let me flee.

The lightning cracks and shrieks above me,
    As the demon crawls slowly near,
    A whimper escapes my trembling body,
    Tonight, alone, I surrender to fear.

White Flag

Please just get me out of here,
Why is this world so hard to love?
I'm waving my white flag in the air,
Eventually, push will come to shove.

I'm doing my best to hold it together,
But Life insists on breaking me apart.
I'm trying so hard to keep it together,
Why does Life always rip me apart?

Please, I beg you, rescue me,
I've tried so hard to save myself,
But if you're there, if you can hear me,
This is my plea for help.

Good Days

Today was a good day. I woke up and only snoozed my alarm clock once. My breakfast was simple—just a bowl of cereal—but this time, I ate it all. I showered. For the first time in weeks, the water felt light and refreshing like it was washing the shadows away.

I met with friends and we chatted and laughed. They said they were worried because I hadn't returned any calls. They said they were glad I had asked to meet. They were glad I was okay. The sun felt warm on my skin and my mind was as clear as the soft blue sky.

I wonder how many good days I'll get this time.

Sometimes, my mind clears and it's not as hard to do all the simple things I'm supposed to do, like eat and sleep and shower and laugh. Until there comes a day when my mind shuts off like switching the light off in a room. That darkness settles, spreading and consuming.

But what scares me most of all is how each time, it gets harder to turn the light back on.

Prey

Block it out, block it out,
I tell myself every day.
And every night I fall asleep
Whispering, *"you're okay."*
But I'm standing on the edge now,
All I need is one more step.
I'm tangled in the shadows like
A fly caught in a spider's web.

Blind

There is a girl who doesn't sleep much. She stays awake because at night, the mask disappears. In the silence of the night, when the world is asleep, that's when she has nothing to fear.

Unbeknownst to the world, that girl is slowly going blind. Blind from the tears she cries. Blind from the smiles that never reach her eyes. Blind from the lies that glare on every side. Blind from the pain of every *"I'm fine"*.

That girl prefers the night because then, she doesn't have to hide. She doesn't have to pretend to see the silver lining or pretend she sees the sun shining. At night, that girl doesn't have to pretend she's alive.

Options

On the top of a mountain,
> Take one step and maybe I'll fly.

On the edge of a cliff,
> Spread my wings and cross the line.

In the corner with arms
> Wrapped to keep me from falling apart.

In the depths of the ocean,
> A soothing way to depart.

On the bed, eyes glazed,
> Cross my heart and hope to die.

It was end, it was blood
> That would mark the grave I lie.

Limbo

I walk among the crowd, but I see nothing, I hear nothing, I know not where I am going. My feet merely walk the familiar path on their own as my mind, my soul, my spirit is floating around elsewhere, floating in limbo.

I recognize joy and sadness, I can differentiate anger and grief, but I feel nothing. I live a half-life, a life of shallow laughter that falls silent to my ears, a life of pretending to see colors that have faded from my colorblind eyes.

To the world, I am living happily, but inside I know I died a long time ago.

Mind vs Body

This heart keeps beating,
Constantly, ceaselessly—
This heart keeps trying to stay alive.

But this brain keeps begging,
Shrieking, slashing—
This brain keeps begging for its demise.

These lungs keep breathing,
Inhale, exhale—
These lungs keep breathing to survive.

But this mind keeps bleeding,
Viciously, endlessly—
This mind keeps bleeding, trying to die.

Wake Me Up

Wake me up when pain is no longer all I know,
When happiness reigns and the tears don't flow,
When haunted eyes cease to shadow this face,
And I don't want to run away from this place.

When hoping doesn't hurt more than it heals,
When it's okay to dream for it's okay to feel,
When words don't stab or cause me to bleed,
When your heart isn't heavy at the sight of me.

When the loneliness and heartache subside,
When a smile doesn't equal a thousand cries,
When the fight is over and enough is enough,
That is when I want you to wake me up.

White

Our bodies burned a brilliant gold,
But nobody heard us scream.

The axe glinted sharp and cold,
But nobody heard us scream.

Our writhing limbs set the sky alight,
But nobody heard us scream.

The world burned until it turned white,
And nobody heard us scream.

Misery

Do you really love me?
>Am I someone you truly need?
>Or would you simply miss me
>If I was missing from your routine?

Do you really care
>About the me that I am?
>Or do you just keep coming back,
>Because you know that you can?

Do you see me as a child—
>Inexperienced and naïve?
>One whose heart you hold in your palm,
>To wield and play with as you please?

Do you even feel remorse
>For all the agony you spew?
>Still, will I ever have the courage
>To walk away from you?

The World She Tore Apart

Stab me now
With that sharp thing
There! Hurry!
For so long I've been dying—

But remember to leave
So they can see
The letter on the table
Saying it wasn't their fault.

Open your eyes!
Do you see the tears,
The broken hearts?
Do you see the world
you tore apart?

But remember to leave
So they can see
The letter on the table
Saying it wasn't their fault.

Please make it end
And take me
To a better place
Than reality—

And I'll remember to leave
So they can see
The letter on the table
Saying it wasn't their fault.

Little One

In the corner, the little one stares back.
Under the blankets, her little heart beats fast.

Her little legs, wobbly at best,
Are drawn up to her face.

Her eyes, shiny underground pools,
Do not belong in this place.

A soft whimper escapes her lips,
Chapped and speckled blue.

Hush, little one, and rest your head,
It'll all be over soon.

Something, Anything

One reminder that happiness is real,
That's all I need tonight.

One reminder that I can heal,
That I'm going to be alright.

I just need something, anything
To help me hold on tonight.

But all I'm grasping at is nothing,
I can't remember what happiness feels like.

Is It Enough…?

Is it enough for the blood to flow in a river,
Glowing under the moonlit sky?
Is it enough to want, to yearn, to desire,
To spread your wings and fly?

Is it enough to charge out into the rain,
Screaming to the heavens above?
Is it enough to try again and again,
To stop hurting all those you love?

Is it enough to send your pleas away,
On the back of a whispering wind?
Is it enough to kneel here day after day,
Begging for your life to begin?

Is it enough to feel the pulse of your heart,
Beating against your fist?
Is it enough to let yourself fall apart,
But trudge on through the mist?

Is it enough to gather the heavy tears,
And stack them to the sky?
Is it enough to let go of all your fears,
And spread your wings and fly?

Buried Words

I wanted to be poetry,
But with him I was a blank page.
My words withered and wilted,
Locked in a pitch-black cage.

With every flick of his wrist,
His pen cut into my veins.
He used me for my blood,
Until I lay there, drained.

When the last drop dripped
Into the stanzas of his poetry,
He sealed me in my crypt,
And my words died with me.

Love & Pain

"Leave me alone," Love spat as she curled up on the couch.

Pain silently refilled Love's glass of wine.

"I said, leave me alone!" Love dissolved into choking sobs. She wrapped her arms around herself for protection. With a gentle touch of his finger, Pain shattered the shield like glass.

"Why won't you leave me alone?" There was no energy left in her words. Her heart pumped desperately to keep her alive.

"You know I can't, Love. Please stop fighting me." Pain reached over to tuck a strand of hair away from Love's soft skin. *"Let me help you."*

Love trembled as she let Pain envelop her in his embrace.

"When this is all over Love, you'll be stronger than you ever thought possible."

Double Homicide

What if we pulled the trigger for each other,
Would they help us then?

When our brains are splattered on the walls,
A pistol in each hand,
Would they realize all we wanted
Was someone to be our friend?

Or would they call us selfish
For such a heinous plan?
To be honest, it's hard to care
When we're crippled by the pain,

When we're screaming in between our sobs,
Again and again and again,
But if we help each other,
Then the torment will finally end,

So what if we helped each other,
What if we made it end?

My Suicide

I will never be the person who cuts herself,
Or hangs herself,
Or jumps off a bridge into the ocean.

I will never overdose on sleeping pills,
Or risk my life for a reckless thrill,
Or take a gun to my head.

But sometimes,
When I cross the street after looking both ways
I pray for a car barreling out of nowhere
To help me disappear.

Sometimes,
When I close my eyes in bed at night
I pray not to wake, to stay asleep the next day
To let the shadows carry me away.

I will never be the person who commits suicide,
But if I were caught between life and death,
If I had to fight to stay alive,
I am the person who would lie down,
Smile, and wait to die.

No More

I don't want to cry anymore.
I don't want to explain anymore.
I don't want their eyes looking at me anymore
Like I'm a freak on display in the circus.

I don't want to hear them whisper anymore,
That they don't know what to do with me.
I don't want to see them tiptoeing anymore,
Like I'm a void that will suck them in
If they get too close.

I don't want to pray for strength anymore,
Or ask for forgiveness anymore.
I don't want to be scared anymore
Of the thoughts that run through my head,
Over and over and over,
Scared of a brain I can't control.

I don't want to cry myself to sleep anymore,
Or hurt anymore.

I don't want to…anymore.

I Wish...

I wish you held my hand
Because it was held out for you,
And I wish you'd let me understand
That you were hurting too.

I wish I read more closely
All the clues you left behind,
If you knew how you have helped me,
Could I have helped you too in kind?

But most of all, I wish your soul
Broken and cracked it was with pain,
Is resting now at peace and whole
And that you never hurt again.

When My Sister Drank Poison

I stared at her rolling eyes,
While her hand in mine turned cold as ice.
I stared at the foam gurgling at her lips,
At the poison she didn't swallow drip, drip, drip.

Her bracelet broke and one by one,
The beads clattered as they came undone.
There was a note, written so neatly,
Signed with tears, planned so completely.

Next to her note laid her favorite pen,
She had once regarded as her closest friend.
I remember how they made stories dance,
How the words twirled as if in a trance.

But now her pen just laid there still,
As if it too had given up all will.
This can't be happening, I remember thinking,
As the room around me just kept shrinking.

That's when I uttered the first painful cry,
When I shook her and I yelled, *"You can't die!"*
I yelled and I yelled as the tears poured out,
"Wake up!" I could do nothing but shout.

Then as if she really did hear me,
As if all she could do was say she was sorry,
A little teardrop fell from her eye,
A teardrop that quietly whispered goodbye.

In that moment, in all my anger,
I realized I couldn't stay angry at her.
Because behind her mask and behind her smile,
I knew her heart had been bleeding awhile.

So, I wiped her tear and I squeezed her hand,
I leaned in close and whispered, *"I understand."*
The last thing I realized as I watched her sleep,
Was that I had never seen her so at peace.

A Mirrored Life

I gave her the blade, I sharpened it twice.
I dipped it in poison, she didn't put up a fight.

Our reflections glinted off the knife,
She walked away, she didn't put up a fight.

I shrieked, *"You coward! You promised!"*
I swung back my arm and I raised a fist.

She braced herself as the mirror shattered,
Speckled with blood as the pieces scattered.

I sank to my knees and she knelt beside me.
"I'm sorry, I can't," she said. *"You see,*

You may be empty, but I have more to give.
So please don't give up yet. I still want to live."

The Choice

On the bathroom floor,
Glass shard in hand,
It catches the light,
Is this the end?

And the tears, they
Bounce off the glass.
Shutting my eyes, I'll
Just make this fast.

What of the dreams
I've yet to dream?
What of the world
I've yet to see?

I lift the shard
Away from my skin.
This night, I choose
To breathe and begin.

A Place to Start

A flickering candle still casts light.
A lonesome star still shines at night.
"And I will fight with all my might,
For I am resilient," whispered my heart.
"All I need is a place to start."

Take Care

She was tired of their fake concerns,
And promises that weren't true.
But with every disappointment,
She learned a lesson too—

That despite what they believed,
She was more capable than they knew.
So she vowed to her reflection,
"From now on, I'll take care of you."

Baby Steps

First step—
Open my eyes.

Second step—
Sit up in bed.

Third step—
Place one foot
On the ground.

Fourth step—
Swing the other
Foot around.

Fifth step—
Maybe four steps are plenty today.
I curl back under the covers
And close my eyes.
After all, four was one more step than yesterday.

Day by Day

How do wings grow?

My wings grow a little more every day. They're
warm, as if they're wrapped in glowing embers.
They glisten with teardrops that cling to every
curve. They're soft like snowflakes, shivering with
every touch.

I have learned that wings are not easy to grow.
They need to be light enough to ride on the wind
and strong enough to carry me far away. So I grow
my wings, day by day.

Silakbo

First, the painful tears
White hot and angry, like glass
Shards set on fire.

Then, the shouts so loud
They trembled the flimsy walls
And shoved us apart.

Last, came the silence
So still, I thought the world was
Holding a long breath.

That was the moment
My road diverged in two and
I chose my future.

The Painting

Her cries poured through him like paint through wispy paper. She begged for escape, but no one came to save her.

She tensed before his raised hand. The swirls of purple and blue hues on her skin pulsed, contorting in a morbid dance.

In the seconds his hand needed to slice through her cries, she saw her colorful self reflected in his eyes.

It was a mumble, barely a whisper. It was enough to freeze his hand in midair.

"Enough." She would no longer be his canvas.

Rainbow

Red for all the anger I kept inside,
Yellow for all the times I was confused,
Blue for all the silent tears I cried,
Purple for all the stars in every bruise.

Red for all the love you could not kill,
Yellow for all the sunshine I could still feel,
Blue for the times you could not break my will,
Purple for all the stars when the bruises healed.

One Day, I Woke Up

Some days, the heat of your skin beside me
Was all the warmth I got.
Some days, I swore I'd always need you
Until the day I did not.

Changed

"I've changed," I murmured that night
To my reflection glinting in the light,
The light that refused to hide my scars,
My scars that shone like purple stars.

"Yes, you have and truly I'm impressed,
How you wear your pain like a little black dress,
Darling, I admit I never knew
That change would look so good on you."

A Bouquet of Snowflakes

Bundled with clear string,
So cold to the touch it stings,
    Lie a bouquet of snowflakes.

Adorned with crystalline tears,
Sharp to the touch, I no longer fear
    Anything you throw my way.

For a trail of white petals I leave behind,
A trail of tears frozen with time,
    I dare you, come whisk me away.

Come hold my hand as I collect,
Every memory, cold and wet,
    And tuck them in my bouquet.

Phoenix

They beat her down
To make her afraid.
They set her aflame
To make her obey.

She never flinched
As she burned like the sun,
As she turned to dust
And they thought they'd won.

She rose from the ashes,
They were wrong to silence her—
You can't kill a woman
Who was born from fire.

Irrepressible

I am not fragile—
> You do not have to wrap me
> In layers of paper to protect me
> From shattering into pieces
> If you accidentally drop me.

I am not broken—
> I will not deny my bruises,
> But you can save all your excuses
> Of how my spirit is defeated, for I
> Am simply a soul who sometimes loses.

I am not delicate—
> I am smarter than your cleverest lie,
> And I will not allow you to crucify
> Me for the way I choose to live,
> And only I decide how I will die.

The Wind

The greatest feeling I ever felt
Was the wind beneath my wings,
So even though you think they're strange
And even though your dislike stings,
I will keep these wings you hate
And you can keep your useless things.

Sidewalk Flower

I don't particularly like growing on this sidewalk.

The concrete obstructs my roots and the metal gates shut me out from the sun's nourishing rays. Life, however, is about being stuck somewhere you never asked to be stuck in and making the best of it.

Some people make it a little harder to be positive, like the naughty child who marched up to me this morning and ripped a leaf from my stem. I flinched in pain, but they only saw me swaying in an absent breeze. Nobody knew it hurt when they plucked off my leaves or petals because nobody ever saw my pain.

Some people make it a little easier, like the curious child who picked up my ripped leaf and exclaimed, *"this is the most perfectly formed leaf ever!"* I beamed with pride knowing even my broken pieces were beautiful.

No, I don't particularly like this sidewalk—

But I make the best of it.

Bully

You thought you could kill me?
With your words as sharp as knives
And the venom dripping from your lies,
Well I'm sorry to disappoint,
But I won't roll over and die.

Who Do You See?

I dare you to look at me—
Tell me, who do you see?
A girl who will obey,
Meek and harmless like prey,
A girl always willing to agree?

Or a girl unafraid to defy,
A girl who refuses to lie,
Come a little closer—
Tell me, can you see her?
Look me right in the eye.

Attempted Robbery

They tried to steal her wings,
  but they didn't know—
They didn't know her wings
  were carved in her bones.

They thought her wings
  were made of glass,
They didn't know her wings
  were made to last.

They tried to steal her wings,
  and for that they paid—
They paid dearly and nearly
  did they not walk away,

For her wings were hard-earned
  and harder than steel,
And she'd fought too hard
  to cower and kneel.

The Last Crazy Night

Banging my head against the wall,
I'm screaming out in pain again.
Wanting so desperately to forget it all,
It's another crazy night again.

Day after day of keeping it together,
Because what's the use of falling apart?
Enough is enough, the chains have severed,
You will no longer play with this broken heart.

Not one second longer will I lose sleep,
I'm taking back the tears I gave,
But this knife you've plunged in me I'll keep,
You will not bury me in this grave.

Cure

There is no cure for my illness, no sword sharp
enough to slay this dragon, no enchantment
powerful enough to exorcise these demons. But
that does not mean I have to surrender.

If these voices insist on taking residence in my
mind, then I will put them to use. I will turn their
shrieks into stanzas, pour their shadows onto
paper and carve verses, inky and black.

Together, we will create art from the darkness.

Armor

No matter how many weapons
Of misery you wield,
With this pen as my sword
And these words as my shield,
I will never die, I will never yield.

The sun is rising in this war,
And you have no power anymore.

Guidance

Sometimes, I look around and realize I'm lost. I wander without aim or direction. I stare, unsure of my own reflection. Sometimes, the world is dark and all I have to guide me are the stones and shards I feel beneath my feet. It's dreary, it's bleak, and sometimes my gaze is etched in defeat.

But I never stop.

Because sometimes there's a flower, a yellow daffodil by a whispering stream. Sometimes, I dip my toes and sigh as the cool water caresses my feet. Sometimes, there's a bird chirping a familiar tune, flapping in step with me. And sometimes, there's the moon illuminating the way for a moment, as if to say, *"You'll know the way even when I fade. You'll know the way."*

The Most Important Thing

Maybe it's a song you've waited to listen to,
Or a book you've waited to read.
Maybe it's admiring how your tears glisten too,
When they fall on your arm like little beads.

Maybe it's the next episode of that TV show
That won't air for another week.
Maybe it's the way the stars are aglow,
The way they tease magic and mystique.

Maybe it's the voice of someone you love,
Whose world would stop without you.
Maybe it's a beautiful memory of
A time when life still felt brand new.

Whatever it takes for you to survive,
However insignificant you think it is,
You hold onto it because if it keeps you alive,
Then it's the most important thing there is.

Between The Lines

I write for those like me
Who can read between the lines,
Who mask behind sunny smiles,
Dark and shadowed minds.

I write for those like me
Who can read between the lines,
Whose hearts have known true pain
And so their souls are kind.

I write for those like me
Who can read between the lines,
So they know they're not alone
If they ever need help to shine.

Dear Darling

You saw the world through rosy eyes,
Before clouds of smoke took over.
Life was shiny like colored glass,
Until like glass it shattered.

You fought to make sense of the pain
That plagued your day and night.
Until there you were, on the ground
Exhausted from the fight.

My darling, it is okay
To look at yourself and forgive.
Won't you use that beautiful heart
To love yourself and live?

Asset

It's okay to feel the good
And the bad pumping through your veins.
You don't have to be immune
To hopeful dreams or overwhelming pain.
Your heart is not a weakness.

My Happy Poem

I wanted to write a happy poem
About sunshine or rainbows or falling in love,
But try as I might and try I did,
My happiest was simply not happy enough.

My sunshine drowned under the pouring rain,
It drenched my rainbow and told it to hide,
And Cupid sent his arrows a different way,
Just when I thought he was on my side.

I wanted to write a lift-me-up poem—
The kind you'd read when you had a bad year,
A poem to remind you you're not alone,
A poem that said what you needed to hear.

But that poem crashed, albeit spectacularly,
Even though I channeled all the joy I had.
I guess sometimes you just need a poem
That tells you it's okay to be sad.

Wrong Love

I knew the first time I saw the curve of his smile,
I knew the first time our fingers intertwined,
From the way the butterflies stayed awhile,
And the tingles when his lips touched mine.

I knew from the sweet whisperings,
The soft kisses and gentle strokes on my arm,
All the times he held my gaze lingering,
And all the promises I would never be harmed.

I knew he was wrong for me from the very start,
I knew I was crazy for wanting him anyway,
I knew I was letting him break my heart,
I knew I'd always be the one to walk away.

Most of all, I knew that when the pain waned,
I would always be strong enough to love again.

Three Gifts

His gift to me came threefold—

First, the soft whisperings
Of the wind dancing
Through the trees brushing
Against the windowpane
As our bed grows cold.

Second, the rose petals
Littering the wooden floor
Like casualties of war
The blood-red and broken
Remnants of us.

Last, a heart that grew strong
After years of being wronged
A heart that finally learned
It never needed him
All along.

Underneath

When all you saw were sunshine and smiles,
It was him who saw the dark and the wild,
And although you promised me you'd stay,
It was him my pain didn't scare away.

So keep your words of how you missed
Your happy one-sided memories,
Because my heart fell in love with his
When he hugged the shadows within me.

You Asked Me Why

Because you saw the sadness in my eyes,
When everyone else laughed with me.

Because you heard the loneliness in my steps,
When everyone else walked with me.

Because when I could bleed no more
From the wounds of this life
You approached me, battered and sore,
And lent me your strength to once again try.

Beautiful

I walked past a girl this morning with gashes creasing her wrists. The sleeves of her sweater were rolled up to her elbows, allowing the sun to illuminate every faded pink line. I asked her why and she said, *"my scars tell the story of what I've been through, and most importantly, show that my story did not end."*

I walked past a girl this afternoon with faded bruises on her skin, patches of light yellow and pale green up and down her body. Her sunflower-patterned skirt fluttered around her knees, allowing her colorful legs to soak in the warmth. I asked her why and she said, *"my scars are a map of the life I was strong enough to live, a constellation of cruelty reminding me of what's behind and lighting the way to a better life ahead."*

I walked past a girl just now, while the sun was setting over the horizon. As blazing orange deepened to red, I saw the shadows swirling underneath the girl's smooth skin. Her heart pumped under layers of scabbed tissue from years of being ripped open, healed, and then ripped open again. I whispered to her, *"your scars are proof of all you've overcome, proof you fought to* stay alive. Your scars are beautiful for they are where your strength lies, so embrace them, honor them, and let them remind you, you did not die."

Bleeding Lines

I never saw her soul through her eyes—
       They were thick opera curtains,
       Never allowing light to pierce through.

But light always finds a way—
       Illuminating her veins to her fingertips,
       Until every word breathed anew.

That is how I learned to read her soul—
       Hidden in the light of her bleeding lines,
       Every word whispering,
       "I've been looking for you."

Difference

When all I knew was solitude
Because the nights stretched on endlessly,
You stayed awake and talked with me.

When all I could do was beg for escape
From this downward spiral asylum cell,
You fought to drag me back from Hell.

When I desperately wanted to let go,
You held on and gave me a reason,
And that has made all the difference.

Above All

I was so young yet so broken,
A free spirit free falling,
Suffocated by emotions,
Always felt, but never spoken.

I am older now yet still
Learning to fly as I fall,
A stronger spirit, a stronger will,
And still breathing, above all.

The Warmest Light

This corpse was lying on the ground,
Frozen cold with blue-black toes,
Never expecting to be found,
Content to slowly decompose.

This boy walked by with jet-black hair,
And beams of gold in his veins.
He could not bear to leave her there,
So he gathered the pieces that remained.

Piece by piece, he warmed her soul,
Setting aflame the shadows inside.
He shared his brightest beams of gold,
And brought this cold corpse back to life.

Kintsugi

That girl was a thousand shattered pieces on the floor, half-alive for so long even her blood flowed gray. Tossed aside and left to die, that girl could not lie to herself another day.

"I am broken, this I admit, with not much left to give. But there is still worth in me, I believe I still deserve to live."

A rivulet of gold trickled towards her, lifting the scattered fragments of her. The glittering liquid embraced each piece, binding her back together until her cracks glinted in the sun, once again whole.

That girl whose blood flowed dull gray now radiated vibrant gold.

The 100th Day

1st day was screaming in a soundproof room—
      Buried alive in my silent tomb.

2nd day was setting the world on fire—
      Memories burning on a pyre.

3rd day was floating with nowhere to go—
      In a crimson river as cold as snow.

100th day—
      I'm starting to feel okay.

No

They said—
Write poetry that shatters glass ceilings,
So all the little girls who come after
Can dance on the shards and use it for art.

They said—
Write poetry that rings in people's ears,
Like freedom bells tolling in the night
Each gong reverberating in their hearts.

They said—
Write poetry that sparks a million dreams,
That imbues color in a colorless world
And heals a reality ripped apart.

But I said—
No.
You will not choose
Whose blood flows through these words
Or
Whose hopes leave footprints behind these lines.
You will not dictate my art.

Confession

I'm sorry, I tried
    To never make you cry,

I'm sorry, I yelled
    When you only meant well,

I'm sorry, I ran
    Away from your hand,

I'm sorry, I broke
    Years of trust turned to smoke,

I'm sorry, I know
    I'm not what you hoped,

I'm sorry, I'm here
    And I won't disappear,

But please, understand
    You can't change who I am,

And I hope that you
    Will one day embrace me too.

A Girl I Knew Once

I think I knew a girl once.
          Grasping at wisps of memory
          I can see her, sad and weary
          And if you ask me to describe her,
          I can say only this—

When she cries,
She cries because she's been strong,
A moment of relief for moments too long.
When she falls,
She always falls too hard,
Hitting the cement, irreparably scarred.

When she smiles,
It's a smile that's looking for light
To guide her way through another night.
When she laughs,
She laughs so no one else feels the pain,
Then she closes her eyes and does it all again.

Yes, I knew a girl once,
          And if you ask me where she is now
          Or if her heart is any lighter
          Or if she's happier somehow
          I can say only this—

Tears still fall from that girl's eyes,
But joy more often fills her days.
Her scars are proof that she survived
A life of darkness, a stifling haze,
Proof she is stronger than any pain,
Then she closes her eyes and does it all again.

Where I Belong

Sometimes life gets in the way,
Sometimes it's just me.
Sometimes I blink
And a day fades to many.

Loud voices that quiet to whispers,
Vivid hues that dull to grey,
Always a sense of something missing
Something lost and gone astray.

But never, it seems, can I forget,
Never can I ignore,
The empty page, the growing itch,
The voices that implore.

Sometimes I lose my way
And everything comes out wrong.
Sometimes I vow never to come back,
Like this isn't where I belong.

But it's here I found solace
It's here I watched fears burn.
It's here I learned to begin again,
And it's here I will always return.

How to Remember Me

Do not portray me with only beauty,
I did not live to be known as pretty.
Do not speak and fail to mention my flaws,
I did not live to hear only applause.

Remember I was both spiteful and kind,
My heart was generous but sometimes blind.
Remember my stumbles, how hard I worked,
And how I struggled to believe my worth.

You can paint a girl with light in her gaze,
And deliver all your speeches of praise,
But do not lie and say I had no pain,
When I fought my darkness time and again.

Do not assert what you wish to be true,
For I did not live to satisfy you.

Darkness, My Old Friend

I used to cower in fear before you,
        Flashlight trembling in my hands,
        Flickers of light swinging back and forth
        At every little sound.

I used to be terrified at the thought of you,
        Of the unseen lurking within you,
        Of the heavy shadows suffocating me,
        As I curl up on the ground.

I still have nights that go on too long,
        Nights that claw at my throat,
        Nights that squeeze until even the stars
        Disappear from my eyes.

But now when I feel your shadows creep near,
        I no longer shudder or shake in fear,
        I accept you for I am stronger now
        And together we will rise.

A Single Teardrop

A single teardrop fell from the sky.
It tumbled through the air.
It fell onto my hand and surprised me,
When it stayed quite still there.

I peeked into the teardrop
And gasped at what I saw—
Beautiful tales of suffering and dreams,
Of life and all its flaws.

It told stories of sadness and hope,
Stories of yearning to be free.
It told stories of proving people wrong
And of making your own destiny.

Then the teardrop became a small puddle,
As if it had no more to say.
Another teardrop fell from the sky,
And on it went in this way.

Now whenever I happen to see
Teardrops falling from the sky,
I always stop to gaze and listen
To all the stories hidden inside.

Tick Tock

Some days go on for eternity,
The ticking clock the soundtrack
Of our nightmares.

Some days slip through our fingers,
As we grasp for the hours
That had just been there.

Some days are perfect,
When we throw regrets into the wind
And lay our souls bare.

But all days end,
So let's all promise to live the day we intend.
Let's never spend any days pretending and
Let's be proud of this life we have penned.

Eternal

Isn't it crazy how something as simple
As a pen and ink and paper and words
Can turn reality upside down
And make the silence be heard?

Isn't it crazy how something as finite
As words and paper and ink and a pen
Can immortalize most anything
And make it last until the end?

Shine

If the world can still shine
After all it's been through,
Then Darling, so can you.

Index

Acknowledgments

To my best friends Fabha Sulthana and Ruby Benitez—thank you for being my first fans, my fiercest supporters, and my safe spaces. This book exists because both of you stubbornly refuse to give up on me.

To my fellow self-published friend Rosemarie Gonzales-Roy—thank you for all your advice and time. I'm thrilled we finally have books beside each other on my bookshelf.

To the rest of my beta-reader friends Maria Salve and Sally Huynh—thank you for your invaluable feedback, which helped shape *Glowstick* into the book it is today.

To my parents and brother—thank you for letting me write for hours and hours and hours.

To you—thank you for reading. I hope you found some comfort in these words. I hope this book was able to be your glowstick in the dark. And I hope you will always remember to shine.

About the Author

Jade M. Wong is the pseudonym of a New York City-based writer, fangirl, and struggling human until further notice.

Jade writes because turning herself into words on a page and learning where she needs to revise and where she's not doing so badly is her medicine for, well, everything. *Glowstick* is the result of her own journey with her mental health.

If Jade were a gazillionaire, she would buy cozy homes in every city she loves. In the meantime, she's making do with cozy corners across the internet. She can be found on social media @JadeMWong and on her website at www.jademwong.com.

Made in the USA
Middletown, DE
12 April 2022

63948847R00071